Gender, Family, and Social Movemen

Sociology for a New Century

A PINE FORGE PRESS SERIES

Edited by Charles Ragin, Wendy Griswold, and Larry Griffin

Sociology for a New Century brings the best current scholarship to today's students in a series of short texts authored by leaders of a new generation of social scientists. Each book addresses its subject from a comparative, historical, and global perspective, and, in doing so, connects social science to the wider concerns of students seeking to make sense of our dramatically changing world.

- *Global Inequalities* York Bradshaw and Michael Wallace
- *Schools and Societies* Steven Brint
- *How Societies Change* Daniel Chirot
- *Ethnicity and Race: Making Identities in a Changing World* Stephen Cornell and Douglas Hartmann
- *The Sociology of Childhood* William Corsaro
- *Cultures and Societies in a Changing World* Wendy Griswold
- *Crime and Disrepute* John Hagan
- *Gods in the Global Village: The World's Religions in Sociological Perspective* Lester R. Kurtz
- *Waves of Democracy: Social Movements and Political Change* John Markoff
- *Development and Social Change: A Global Perspective* Philip McMichael
- *Constructing Social Research* Charles C. Ragin
- *Women and Men at Work* Barbara Reskin and Irene Padavic
- *Cities in a World Economy* Saskia Sassen

Forthcoming:

- *An Invitation to Environmental Sociology* Michael M. Bell
- *Families and Public Policy* Diane Lye
- *Aging and Inequality* Fred Pampel

Gender, Family, and Social Movements

Suzanne Staggenborg

McGill University

PINE FORGE PRESS

Thousand Oaks ◆ London ◆ New Delhi

For information, address:

 Pine Forge Press
A Sage Publications Company
2455 Teller Road
Thousand Oaks, California 91320
(805) 499-4224
E-mail: sales@pfp.sagepub.com

Sage Publications Ltd.
6 Bonhill Street
London EC2A 4PU
United Kingdom

Sage Publications India Pvt. Ltd.
M-32 Market
Greater Kailash I
New Delhi 110 048 India

Production Editor: Sanford Robinson
Production Assistant: Lynn Miyata
Designer: Lisa S. Mirski
Typesetter: Rebecca Evans
Cover: Lisa S. Mirski
Print Buyer: Anna Chin

Printed in the United States of America

98 99 00 01 02 10 9 8 7 6 5 4 3 2 1

Library of Congress Cataloging-in-Publication Data

Staggenborg, Suzanne.
    Gender, family, and social movements / by Suzanne Staggenborg.
        p. cm. — (Sociology for a new century)
    Includes bibliographical references (p.) and index.
    ISBN 0-7619-8516-6 (pbk. : acid-free paper)
    1. Sex role. 2. Social change. 3. Social movements.
  4. Feminism. 5. Family. I. Title. II. Series.
HQ1075.S69 1997
305.3—dc21   97-21060

To Charlie and Laura

Contents

ABOUT THE AUTHOR

Suzanne Staggenborg received her Ph.D. from Northwestern University in 1985. She taught at Indiana University in Bloomington before joining the faculty of McGill University in Montreal, Canada, where she is currently Associate Professor of Sociology. Her published work includes *The Pro-Choice Movement: Organization and Activism in the Abortion Conflict* (1991), and a number of articles about abortion politics and social movements. She is currently studying the development of the women's movement and movement-countermovement dynamics. She and her husband, Rod Nelson, have two children, Charlie and Laura.

ABOUT THE PUBLISHER

Pine Forge Press is a new educational publisher, dedicated to publishing innovative books and software throughout the social sciences. On this and any other of our publications, we welcome your comments and suggestions.

Please call or write to us at:

Pine Forge Press
A Sage Publications Company
2455 Teller Road
Newbury Park, CA 91320
(805) 499-4224
E-mail: sales@pfp.sagepub.com

Visit our new World Wide Web site, your direct link to a multitude of on-line resources: http://www.sagepub.com/pineforge

Foreword

Sociology for a New Century offers the best of current sociological thinking to today's students. The goal of the series is to prepare students, and in the long run, the informed public, for a world that has changed dramatically in the last three decades, and one that continues to astonish.

This goal reflects important changes that have taken place in sociology. The discipline has become broader in orientation, with an ever growing interest in research that is comparative, historical, or transnational in orientation. Sociologists are less focused on "American" society as the pinnacle of human achievement and more sensitive to global processes and trends. They also have become less insulated from surrounding social forces. In the 1970s and 1980s sociologists were so obsessed with constructing a science of society that they saw impenetrability as a sign of success. Today, there is a greater effort to connect sociology to the ongoing concerns and experiences of the informed public.

Each book in this series offers in some way a comparative, historical, transnational, or global perspective to help broaden students' vision. Students need to comprehend the diversity in today's world and to understand the sources of diversity. This knowledge can challenge the limitations of conventional ways of thinking about social life. At the same time, students need to understand that issues that may seem specifically "American" (for example, the women's movement, an aging population bringing a strained social security and health care system, racial conflict, national chauvinism, and so on) are shared by many other countries. Awareness of commonalities undercuts the tendency to view social issues and questions in narrowly American terms and encourages students to seek out the experiences of others for the lessons they offer. Finally, students need to grasp phenomena that transcend national boundaries—trends and processes that are supranational (for example, environmental degradation). Recognition of global processes stimulates student awareness of causal forces that eclipse national boundaries, economies, and politics.

One of the most remarkable developments of the twentieth century, especially the second half, has been broad changes in gender relations and consciousness. In *Gender, Family, and Social Movements*, Suzanne Staggenborg charts these changes and explores their larger social contexts. Two crucial features of her approach make the treatment of gender unique and powerful. First, she looks at gender relations within the context of the family and the many changes it has endured. Rather than seeing gender as involving relations between men and women and nothing more, she sees it as part of a complex of social forces that have had a powerful impact on how families are made and unmade. Second, the author emphasizes the collective struggle and overt conflict that has accompanied changes in gender relations. Many of the most important social movements of the late twentieth century have concerned gender or the family in one way or another. Further, these movements have raised the gender consciousness of many, often in opposite directions. A complex interplay of consciousness and action has unfolded in social movements and counter social movements in several key social arenas—equal rights, abortion, and sexual orientation. Staggenborg's portrait of gender, the family, and social movements at century's end shows that the political struggles linked to changing gender relations will not soon diminish.

Preface

The topics of "gender" and "social movements" have each received a great deal of scholarly attention in recent years, yet explicit attention to the connections between the two phenomena is just beginning. The subject matter is potentially vast, and this book does not attempt to provide a comprehensive discussion of gender and social movements. Instead, I focus on the relationship between social movements and gender relations associated with the family. My aim is to look at some interesting ways in which gender and social movements interact in the context of family relations. I hope that the work will stimulate thinking about other connections and issues that must necessarily be omitted from a short book.

There are two general types of questions involved in looking at the connections between gender and family relations and social movements. First, how have changes in gender and family arrangements affected the rise and development of social movements? Second, how have social movements altered gender and family arrangements? Throughout this book, I show how large-scale changes are important in creating the possibility for new gender relations and the bases for movement mobilization. I also show how social movements are important in generating new gender consciousness and in helping to change men and women.

As important changes occur, there is often conflict around various issues. I consider in detail the intense battles between movements and countermovements that have occurred around the issues of the Equal Rights Amendment, abortion, and gay and lesbian rights. I show how the battles are related to large-scale changes that are affecting individuals and families. For both movements and countermovements, these issues symbolize fundamental values and lifestyle choices. There are important differences between the opposing sides, but also some common concerns related to widespread changes that affect us all.

By linking large-scale changes to current conflicts over issues and the real problems of men, women, and families, the book attempts to bridge the gap between macrohistorical events and interpersonal relations.

Students often have difficulty appreciating macrolevel analyses because they seem too distant and abstract. By showing how large-scale historical transformations are relevant to pressing social issues, I hope to help interest students in macrolevel analysis. With regard to gender, I try to show how gender relations are not simply individual preferences, but are related to institutional structures.

My approach to controversial issues such as abortion and same-sex sexuality is intended to provide students of varying backgrounds and beliefs with a new perspective. We all have our own opinions on various issues, and my purpose here is not to decide which positions are correct. Rather, I want to help students to understand *why* people feel so strongly about these issues. What, for example, are the very real concerns behind fears such as the fear that homosexuals will recruit one's children? The book shows how widespread changes have created real problems, which are sometimes symbolized by concerns over issues such as gay and lesbian rights. We all face new challenges in raising children, managing work and family, and creating new possibilities for men and women. As concerned citizens, we all need to think about ways of creating community supports for families and new kinds of structures that enable men and women to make choices about how to live their lives.

I would like to thank Charles Ragin for encouraging me to write this book and for advice along the way. Steve Rutter, the president of Pine Forge Press, also provided very helpful advice and showed great patience in waiting for me to finish the book. Rebecca Smith, the developmental editor for Pine Forge, made numerous editorial improvements in the manuscript and excellent suggestions regarding its development and organization. I thank colleagues and friends who helped in various ways, including Rod Nelson, Brian Powell, Verta Taylor, and Jessie Tzeng. I am particularly grateful to Verta Taylor and to several anonymous reviewers for detailed comments on each chapter. As always, my husband Rod was a source of great personal as well as intellectual support. Our children, Charlie and Laura, did their best to distract me; the book is dedicated to them and to their future.

1

The Interplay of Gender
and Social Movements

Women's lives have changed dramatically over the course of the last two centuries and especially during the last several decades. It wasn't so long ago that women seemed to have little control over their own lives—not even over their own bodies:

> Imagine your best friend confiding in strictest secrecy that she is taking a trip to Puerto Rico to get an abortion, illegal on the U.S. mainland. Another friend enthusiastically tells you about a terrific new minipill that doesn't make you gain weight the way the regular birth control pill does. Your doctor says he'll fit you with a diaphragm after your honeymoon, not before. The obstetrician tells your sister that natural childbirth is kooky and dangerous and that it is better to take a little something to forget what happens. Welcome to 1969. (Boston Women's Health Book Collective 1992)

Since 1969, women have gained a great measure of control over their bodies with the advent of legal abortion, available contraceptives, and the rise of women-oriented health care. These advances owe much to the work of the women's health movement, including the Boston Women's Health Book Collective. At a time when many women were ignorant about their own bodies, this small group of women began to do research on various issues related to women's health. In 1970 they published their findings in what became a best-selling book, *Our Bodies, Ourselves*.

But that was just one part of women's battle. Women's social roles were also seriously circumscribed. Patricia Ireland recalls:

> It seems almost like yesterday. The shrill retort rings clear: "How can they expect me to teach calculus to girls!" All eyes turned to me as I felt myself shrinking in my seat. The outburst of my freshman calculus professor was in response to what I thought was a reasonable question about a math problem. I never asked another question, got a D in the class, and changed my major from math to education. (Ireland 1992)

Ireland eventually became a lawyer and the president of the largest feminist organization in the United States, the National Organization for Women (NOW).

Everywhere today we see changes in women's social status: in the work they do, in the way they dress, in their sexual activity, in their reproductive choices, in their relationships. Men's lives have also changed, although not quite so dramatically as women's. For both men and women, however, despite real transformations of social structure and culture, significant obstacles to changes in roles and institutions have endured.

This chapter will consider how the experience of being either female or male is connected to social change, especially as change is effected by social movements. I begin by clarifying the meaning of *gender* and then turn to a discussion of social movements, noting some of the ways in which gender arrangements affect movements and some of the influences of social movements on gender relations.

The Meaning of Gender

Gender once referred exclusively to an aspect of language (for instance, the pronouns "he" and "she"), but the term has been appropriated by feminists and scholars to refer to "the social organization of the relationship between the sexes" (Scott 1986). In many societies, for example, women traditionally were expected to take care of children while men earned a living. Note that *gender* is used to refer to arrangements that are socially determined. *Sex*, on the other hand, is used to refer to biologically determined characteristics such as women's capacity for bearing children. In other words, gender arrangements are not the result of "natural" differences between men and women but of social and cultural choices. Although the terms *sex* and *gender* are still used interchangeably at times, the most current usage maintains a distinction between biological and social relations; thus we see the older concept of "sex roles" increasingly replaced by "gender roles."

Early scholarship on gender differences focused on gender roles as attributes of individuals—for instance, how traditional boys' and girls' toys train them for adult gender roles. However, more recent work (for example, Acker 1990; Lorber 1994) has expanded our understanding by recognizing that gender resides not only in individuals but also in organizations and institutions within societies (Whittier, Taylor, and Reger 1995). This reconceptualization of gender is important because it leads to new research questions. Researchers who focus only on the gender roles